The
Fireside
Book
2022

"A friend may be waiting
behind a stranger's face."
– *Maya Angelou*

Contents

Poetry

6 **Rejoice With Nature** *by Iris Hesselden*
9 **New Discoveries** *by John Darley*
10 **Constant Companions** *by Laura Tapper*
13 **Cherry Blossom** *by Carrie Hewlett*
14 **Penpals** *by Sharon Haston*
22 **Bits And Bobs** *by S. Bee*
24 **Soft Rain** *by Eithne Cullen*
26 **The Heron** *by Eileen Hay*
28 **Mummy's Down The Garden** *by Dennis W. Turner*
30 **Acorn To Oak** *by Maggie Ingall*
32 **A Country Lane** *by John Darley*
34 **Friends Old And New** *by Emma Canning*
43 **My Jaunty Blackbird** *by George Hughes*
45 **The Little Things** *by Maggie Ingall*
46 **Strawberry Moon** *by Laura Tapper*
48 **Summer's Swell** *by Heather Walker*
50 **In My Garden Shed** *by Megan Carter*
52 **Summer Healing** *by Iris Hesselden*
54 **Cloud Puffs** *by Lily Christie*
57 **A Holiday Romance** *by John Darley*
65 **Seashells** *by Maggie Ingall*
66 **A Day In The Hills** *by Dennis W. Turner*
69 **A Sea Mist** *by Eileen Hay*
70 **Discovered** *by Laura Tapper*
72 **Rooftop Retreat** *by Marian Cleworth*
75 **Buttercups** *by Lily Christie*
76 **Wish You Were Here?** *by Kathryn Sennen*
84 **A Different World** *by John Darley*

From The Manse Window

16 **Dependable As The Seasons** *by Rev. Andrew Watson*
36 **Sowing The Seeds** *by Janice Ross*
58 **Summer Is Coming** *by Rev. Susan Sarapuk*
78 **Making Memories** *by Maggie Ingall*
100 **A Time Of Renewal** *by David McLaughlan*
120 **Autumn Promises** *by Rev. Susan Sarapuk*
142 **Get Ready For Advent!** *by Rev. Ian W.F. Hamilton*
162 **Keep The Spirit Alive** *by Maggie Ingall*

Nature's Calendar

20 Early Spring
40 Late Spring
62 Early Summer
82 Late Summer
104 Early Autumn
124 Late Autumn
146 Early Winter
166 Late Winter

87 **Farmyard Swallows** *by Dawn Lawrence*
89 **Ken's Bench** *by John Darley*
90 **Autumn** *by Megan Carter*
92 **A Small Miracle!** *by Eileen Hay*
94 **Reading With Toby** *by Kate Bradbury*
96 **Song Of The Harvest** *by Laura Tapper*
98 **The Otter** *by Kenneth Steven*
106 **Out Of This World** *by Angie Keeler*
108 **A Woodland Walk** *by Emma Canning*
110 **The Future Passed . . .** *by John Darley*
112 **A Little Note To Self** *by Emma Canning*
114 **The Stormy Sea** *by Eileen Hay*
116 **"For Sale"** *by Maggie Ingall*
119 **Precious Patchwork** *by Judy Jarvie*
126 **The Silvery Moon** *by Heather Walker*
128 **From The Sky** *by Dawn Lawrence*
130 **Late Autumn** *by John Darley*
132 **Winter Wonderland!** *by Eileen Hay*
135 **Feed The Birds** *by Judy Jarvie*
136 **Second-Hand Home** *by Laura Tapper*
138 **The Choir** *by Judy Jarvie*
140 **The Robin** *by Dave Dutton*
148 **Special Visitor** *by Judy Jarvie*
150 **A Ferry Ride In Winter** *by Eileen Hay*
152 **Rain On Remembrance Day** *by Sharon Haston*
154 **Our Piano** *by Vivien Brown*
156 **Winter In The Churchyard** *by Eileen Hay*
158 **That Secret Ingredient** *by C.P. Nield*
161 **The Lonely Christmas Tree** *by Dave Dutton*
168 **Snow Day** *by Judy Jarvie*
170 **Winter Sunrise** *by Marian Cleworth*
173 **New Year** *by Judy Jarvie*

Illustrations by Manon Gandiolle and Mandy Dixon.

Rejoice With Nature

The lambs are in the meadow,
The buds are on the tree,
And hope is blossoming around –
It's there for you and me.
The daylight growing longer,
The sunshine growing strong,
And all our winter hopes and dreams
Have carried us along.

As we step forward through the year,
The darkness left behind,
New optimism touches souls
And comforts heart and mind.
So as the weeks go slipping by
And time just steals away,
Enjoy the beauty nature gives,
Rejoicing every day.

Iris Hesselden.

New Discoveries

Going for a walk today
I thought I'd go a different way,
Down avenues I hardly know,
Where springtime bulbs begin to show.
Along another unknown street,
Where passing people meet and greet,
And then a park came into view,
So green beneath this sky of blue.
I chose a bench to sit upon,
Feeling warmth where sunlight shone.
It's strange, by changing my routine
And going where I hadn't been,
How life can still, at times, surprise,
And bring new interests to your eyes.
Explorers must have felt the same,
Discovering landscapes with no name.

John Darley.

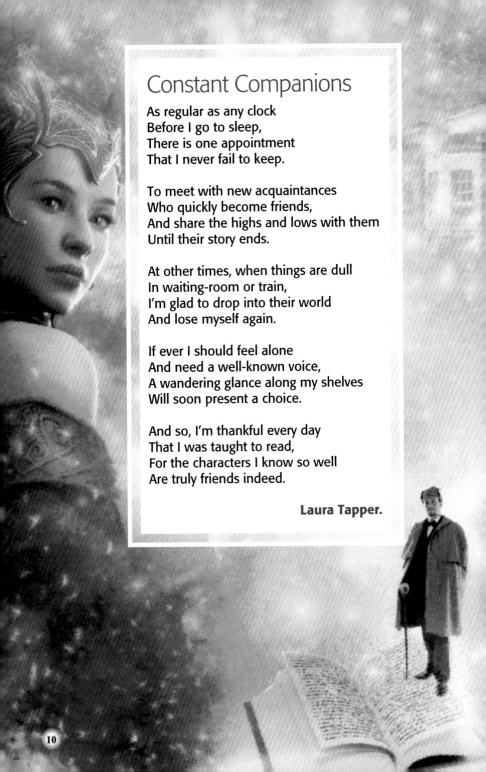

Constant Companions

As regular as any clock
Before I go to sleep,
There is one appointment
That I never fail to keep.

To meet with new acquaintances
Who quickly become friends,
And share the highs and lows with them
Until their story ends.

At other times, when things are dull
In waiting-room or train,
I'm glad to drop into their world
And lose myself again.

If ever I should feel alone
And need a well-known voice,
A wandering glance along my shelves
Will soon present a choice.

And so, I'm thankful every day
That I was taught to read,
For the characters I know so well
Are truly friends indeed.

Laura Tapper.

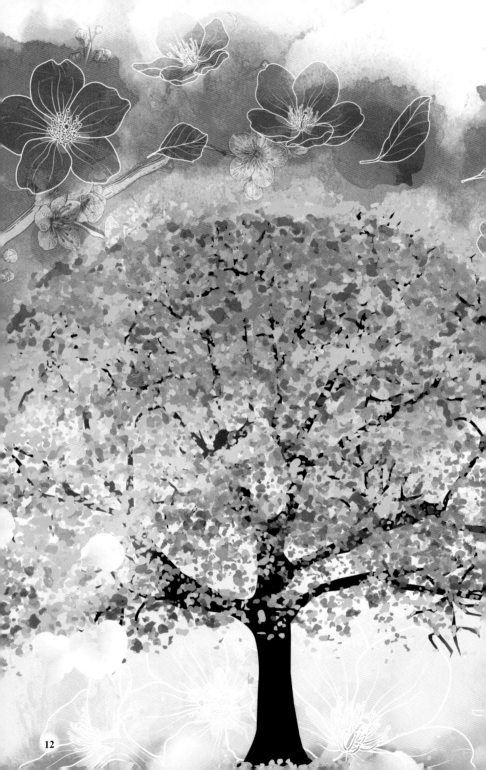

Cherry Blossom

Tender flakes of blossom
Float past me in the air.
The delicate, pure petals,
Darting here and there.

Like flotsam, cherry blossom
Gets strewn across the lawn:
Small pillows of the brightest white
And pinky shades of dawn.

The word for cherry blossom
Is *sakura* in Japanese;
It means to bloom or smile or laugh –
Happiness in the breeze.

And that's just how they make me feel,
Those blessings of springtime,
Bringing hope from Mother Nature,
Her most positive sign.

Carrie Hewlett.

Penpals

I loved receiving letters from friends in different places,
Also seeing photos of their lovely, smiling faces.
Veroni was from Sweden, Dina from the USA,
I wonder what they're up to and what they're doing today.

I would tell them all my news, what was happening at school,
About my happy holidays in wonderful Blackpool.
I'd confide about the boys I liked; did they like me, too?
I cried on to the pages when I had the teenage blues.

I watched out for the postman, longing to hear all their news.
Reading about their exploits would always keep me amused.
I look back with great fondness on the letters that we penned.
I think I'll try to trace them and become their Facebook friend.

Sharon Haston.

from the Manse Window

Dependable As The Seasons

WHEN we were children, there were things we often took for granted: that our parents would feed us, that our teachers knew everything, that Santa would come down the chimney with presents at Christmas!

Over time we learned to say "thank you" when something nice happened to us, because we should be grateful, and it might not always be the case.

We learned to ask questions, because some of the things we were told turned out to be wrong, and nobody knows everything.

We learned to be tough when necessary, because sometimes life gets complicated.

Yet even if some disappointments in growing up can make us cautious or cynical, there are other things which seem set to reassure us. Like the seasons!

Spring follows winter every year, just as day follows night. Every day, in most parts of the world for most of the year, the sun rises, even if it's hidden by cloud, and even if some days it sets again quite quickly.

The moon follows its regular phases repeatedly. The tides ebb and flow. Many stars can be charted as to their exact position on any given day of the year.

It's not a random mess. The cosmos, and particularly this planet, seems precisely ordered to support life.

Imagine if spring didn't follow winter, or if the seasons didn't follow a set pattern but varied in order from year to year.

When would farmers sow seeds? What if winter kicked in before they had a chance to reap a harvest? There might be no daily bread and soon no life on Earth!

Thankfully, spring returns every year. It may be early or late, but it will come around springtime, in between winter and summer.

We can set our calendars, make plans accordingly and watch for the daffodils. There's something very dependable ▶

Shutterstock.

by Rev. Andrew Watson

about that. It seems like a well-designed, faithful system.

Thanks to its rest over winter, come spring the land is ready to nurture new life again.

It blossoms and grows by the warm sun and showers of summer, so that we can harvest in autumn, decorate our church buildings with corn, fruit and vegetables in October, and sing hymns like "Great Is Thy Faithfulness".

Faithfulness is an attribute of God celebrated from the earliest writings in the Bible.

The entire Old Testament and the advent of Christ in the New Testament are the epic unfolding of his covenant made with Abraham and his family in the book of Genesis.

From his rescuing them from slavery in Exodus and settling them in the promised land of Canaan, to preserving them in Babylonian exile and bringing them home to Jerusalem in preparation for the Messiah, centuries of history reveal a story with one consistent thread – God keeping his word to his people.

From a human perspective, world events convulse in dramatic and uncertain ways as human empires and institutions rise and fall.

We may find comfort and hope in the unchanging character of our maker and rescuer: his holiness, his love and his grace.

People can sometimes let us down but – like the spring in springtime – God is faithful!

He is always at work and his plans are good.

It should be reassuring that the one who created such excellent and beneficial natural order has revealed a similar moral order for the benefit of individuals, families and communities.

Through the ages, people all over the world have discovered that when we take this aspect of God's faithfulness seriously we can much better appreciate the other aspects, his love and grace.

Inhabitants of Jerusalem frequently sang psalms of praise and thanksgiving to God for his faithful love to their people.

Jesus developed this thinking further, teaching his followers to trust in God as a loving and generous heavenly father who delighted in giving good gifts to his children.

God is dependable in sending the seasons, the sun and rain on "the good and the evil alike".

He sees the sparrow fall, numbers the hairs of our heads and is careful to provide all the things he knows his children need.

What the New Testament celebrates most is God's grace: how he treats us better than he needs to, and better than we deserve at times.

He is always faithful to his own nature. Though he condemns wrongdoing, he graciously provides a way for people to find forgiveness through Christ.

When our own children were small we tried to encourage them to recognise the order and beauty of nature, and to respond with respect and care.

"This is good," we'd say, "let's not ruin it with litter or waste it foolishly."

Similarly, we taught them that the one who created it all is deserving of reverence and more.

We should love him back for all his loving kindness to us and be ever thankful for his "amazing grace".

Not all lessons learned in childhood let us down. This one is faithful and true!

I took my first faith steps when very young and am happy to testify a lifetime later:

"Great is thy faithfulness, Lord unto me"! ■

Nature's Calendar For *Spring*

The Columbia River Gorge in the United States stretches for 130 km and can be up to 1,200 metres deep. In spring, parts of the surrounding area are covered in sunflowers.

This stunning tunnel avenue of spring blossoms is in Bonn, Germany. Bonn was also the capital of West Germany up until 1991.

The Palouse region of Washington State consists of these hills, created by thousands of years of dust and silt blowing across the plains. As wildflowers and crop flowers come into bloom in spring, they create a display that looks like the Tuscan hills.

Shutterstock.

Spring is the best time of year to watch whales migrate south towards equatorial waters in the northern hemisphere. Around 20,000 head for the warm waters off the Mexican coast alone.

Martenitsi are bracelets made of red and white yarn in Bulgaria. A mythical figure called Baba Marta heralds the end of winter, and bracelets are exchanged on Baba Marta Day on March 1, then hung on bushes at the first sign the wearer sees of spring.

Floriade is a spring celebration in the Australian capital city of Canberra. Running from September to October (spring in the southern hemisphere), it's a riot of colour with flowers on display everywhere.

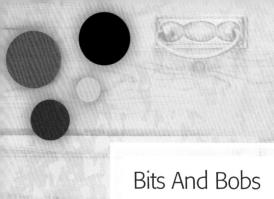

Bits And Bobs

My drawer is bursting with bobs and bits –
I guess it's time to have a blitz.
Instructions for an old computer,
With it, a guide for the new router.

A pack of playing cards, pens galore,
A ball of string, and oh, lots more!
Bags for life, an old screwdriver,
An outdated voucher for a bottle of Tizer.

Rubber gloves and stray drawing-pins,
Assorted recipes, a sticky toffee tin,
A mini torch, a tangled shoelace,
Loose batteries, a spectacles case.

A broken watch, a box of matches,
A sewing kit and fabric patches,
Crumpled envelopes, a tube of glue –
There's lots to clear for me and you!

S. Bee.

Soft Rain

Don't talk to me of April showers;
Show me the lovely springtime flowers:
Gold daffodils and bluebells coming,
Birds so active, insects humming.
Brighter mornings start the day,
Sunshine shakes the blues away.
The soft rain makes a gentle sound,
Seeps in and softens up the ground.

Eithne Cullen.

The Heron

He stood so tense with shoulders hunched
And still as still could be,
His whole attention focused on
The fish that he could see.
But just as he was poised to strike
A walker came in sight,
His panting dog some yards ahead –
Poor heron got a fright!
With screeching cries he flapped away,
Legs dangling in the air;
The dog raced to his master's side
As he, too, had a scare!

Eileen Hay.

Mummy's Down The Garden

Mummy's down the garden and she won't be back just yet.
She's talking to the neighbours and she'll be some time, I'll bet!
I'd like to do some useful things before she comes back in.
Oh, good! This is my lucky day; I've found the rolling-pin!
I've seen some pastry in the fridge; it's just inside the door,
But I can't reach the worktop so I'll roll it on the floor.

Mummy's down the garden and she'll be a little while.
I'm doing things to help her, as I love to see her smile.
I plugged her brand-new iron in and now it's very hot.
I'm doing all the ironing; there's really quite a lot.
The shirts were hard to do, but I've been taking lots of care.
I think they look quite pretty with brown patterns everywhere.

Mummy's down the garden. She's been hours but I don't mind.
There must be something else to do; I'll see what I can find.
There's lots of dirty crockery; I'm clearing it away.
I know that she'll be quite surprised; I wonder what she'll say.
I've washed up all the plates, but they're still wet. I don't know why.
I'll put them into this machine and let them tumble dry.

Mummy's down the garden. She should soon be coming in.
I'll do some baked beans for our tea if I can find the tin.
Oh, here it is! I've found it, but the opener's not here.
I'll have to get a move on as our teatime's getting near.
If I can't find the opener we'll have no tea tonight.
I'll microwave them as they are; ten minutes should be right.

Mummy's down the garden but I can't do any more.
I've tried to tidy up and clean the mess up from the floor.
The problem is the vacuum cleaner doesn't seem to know
That when you plug it in it's meant to suck instead of blow.
I've tried to help my mummy just as best as I know how;
I hope she's pleased about it. Oh, I think that's Mummy now . . .

Dennis W. Turner.

Acorn To Oak

If I should plant an acorn to make a mighty tree,
I wonder just what changes my full-grown oak might see.
I guess no kings or outlaws would hide within its boughs,
Nor yet, beneath its branches, would sleepy milkmaids drowse.
So would it see the launch pads for rockets to afar?
To Mars and back in moments, or perhaps some distant star?
Will messages by thought-waves become our natural state?
Will microchipping humans make all our brains inflate?
And will robotic servants our every need attend?
Ah, well, it's all beyond me – good luck, my little friend.

Maggie Ingall.

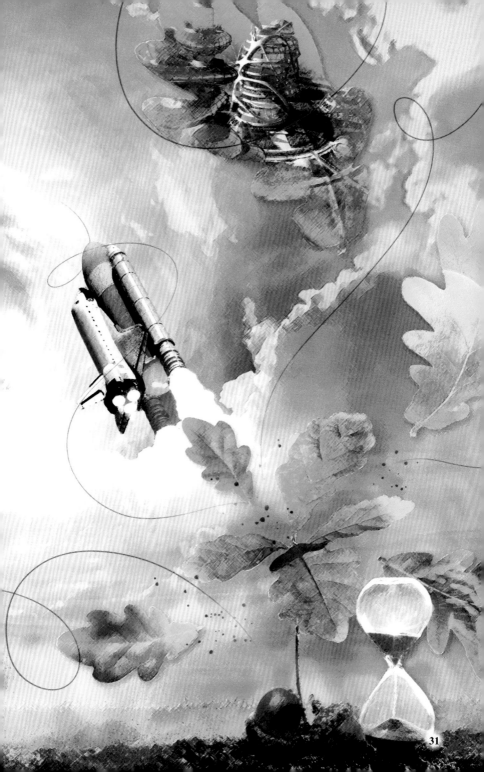

A Country Lane

It's funny how this narrow lane
Provides a broader view;
How this forgotten byway
Only footsteps now pass through.

I once worked in a city
Where the pavements, although wide,
Were always crammed with people,
So I had to step aside.

I now have time to linger,
To stroll at my own pace,
Discovering nature's secrets
And to revel in the space.

All year round there's something
To hear or catch your eye:
A vixen's call in winter
Or the spring's first butterfly.

The lane brings so much pleasure,
It's a peaceful place to be,
And when I'm done it leads me back
To home and family.

John Darley.

Friends Old And New

One happy day, two people meet:
Kind words and smiles exchanged.
A wish to keep in touch expressed;
A second date arranged.

Then phone calls, texts and further plans:
There's laughter, chatter, tea,
And both feel buoyed, at perfect ease
In each other's company.

And weeks stretch into months, then years –
Two lives entwine; souls bared.
There's empathy and loyalty,
Support, and problems shared.

And so fond memories are made
From the things that friends are for . . .
And every old friend once was new –
So take the chance to make one more!

Emma Canning.

Sowing The Seeds

As a child I watched my parents keep a small garden beautifully.

Both my mum and dad tended this area religiously, and I can still picture it and smell it: the scent of the lilac hanging over the wall, the roses climbing up the sandstone frontage, the tubs awash with bright, heavy-headed dahlias.

On the odd day when I felt like helping, the job was always weeding. What could be more boring and backbreaking than weeding? I have disliked the job ever since!

My grandfather, also a keen gardener, had an allotment near the school. I can still see him hoeing the rows of vegetables, the newly turned earth immaculate, with not a weed in sight.

On the odd day when I felt like helping him, the job was still weeding!

There is, I am told, more to gardening than weeding.

In fact, many find it to be a satisfying and therapeutic hobby.

Looking back, my problem was that I was a fair-weather gardener. The garden was the place to be on a warm summer's day. Everything looked beautiful, I might even get a suntan, but the weeds liked to grow in that climate, too!

I was never around when my parents were digging over the ground at the cold back end of the year, or planting in spring. I may have grown to enjoy that!

Most children love getting their hands into good brown soil and planting seeds. For young children, quick results are important to keep their interest fuelled.

Sunflower seeds provide bright and speedy results. There are likely to be few five-year-olds who haven't brought a sunflower seedling home at one time and watched anxiously as it grew taller and taller, hoping that theirs might win the "tallest in the class" competition.

Growing beansprouts in jars and cress for egg sandwiches

Shutterstock.

by Janice Ross

▶ are exciting and rewarding activities, too. As they move on to vegetable and flower seed planting, children learn that not everything sprouts as quickly as these first ones.

Gardeners need to develop patience as they wait for seedlings to grow.

My youngest granddaughter, aged three, has been expecting red tomatoes every day since a kind friend gave her some young plants a few weeks ago.

I do hope the disappointment doesn't dampen her enthusiasm.

Seeds come in all shapes and sizes. Some rainforest orchids have seeds smaller than a pinhead. At the other end of the scale, we have the seed of the palm tree, coco de mer, which is the biggest seed in the world.

This seed can be up to 30 cm (12 ins) long and weigh up to 18 kg (40 lbs). Probably the avocado seed, or pit as it is called, is the biggest we would come across.

All seedlings need water, oxygen and light, but in varying degrees. Cactus plants, used to desert conditions, can survive on very little water, whereas some houseplants simply guzzle it.

Some seeds prefer shallow planting because they need a lot of light to germinate, while some, like fennel seeds, need to be dug in deeply as they prefer total darkness.

Some seeds, like those of the cabbage family, sprout in no time; others, such as peppers and celery, are very slow to germinate.

The common sight of burning heather on our Scottish hillsides reveals that even fire and smoke can encourage new seed germination.

My husband is a keen collector of alpines. These are plants that live at high altitudes in mountainous terrain, usually spending the winter covered by snow and ice.

"Edelweiss", of "The Sound Of Music" fame, is an alpine, as are cobalt-blue gentians and lewisia. These thrive above the tree line in light soil, often in north-facing locations, hugging the ground to keep from being battered by strong winds.

Alpine seeds lie dormant in the soil for months before germinating. In order for a gardener to germinate these kinds of seeds, it's necessary to mimic the conditions they face when breaking from this dormancy in nature.

For years, my husband would gather alpine seeds in autumn and place them in old plastic 35 mm cartridge film boxes. They'd go into the fridge, or sometimes the freezer, for two to three months.

No matter how long the germination process, the purpose of all seeds is to reproduce.

Another of the smallest seeds known is the mustard seed, its diameter measuring only 1-2 mm. It is easy to grow, without the

need for a garden or even soil.

Sprinkle some seeds over some kitchen roll in a shallow container, place on a sunny window-sill and water frequently.

Hey, presto! You are rewarded with a lovely peppery flavour to add to egg sandwiches or a tasty garnish for soup.

Though tiny, mustard seeds can grow into the tallest of garden shrubs, and even into trees in Mediterranean areas.

We read that Jesus taught his disciples an important lesson from this particular seed.

The black mustard, a particularly pungent variety common in Palestine, could grow tall enough even to provide the birds of the air with a place to nest.

Jesus wanted his followers to understand that, although they might feel small and insignificant, like this particular seed, a little bit of faith in God could result in amazing consequences.

Like the seed in his hand, his disciples had within them huge potential to be the reproducers of his love on earth.

Small acts of love and kindness would grow God's kingdom.

All that was needed were the right conditions. He promised that he would help them to that end, by providing love, strength, protection and counsel.

They obviously got the message, because after his death and resurrection their joy and faith resulted in a huge growth in numbers in the early church.

So whenever we grow seeds this year, be it cress seeds or something much larger, may we remember the potential that has been invested in each of us. And, as they say on "Gardeners' Question Time", "Good gardening!" ■

Nature's Calendar For Spring

Ospreys at Chesapeake Bay in the US indicate the health of the waters. They rely on fish, so a decline of the birds shows the need for care to be taken with the area's fish stocks.

Provence is the place to go as the lavender starts to flower in June. Getting there as early in the season as possible is recommended, as the area draws enormous numbers of tourists during the summer.

Over 300 species of bird call the Canadian province of New Brunswick home, and it's a hotspot for spring and autumn migrations.

Shutterstock.

It's time for the bumblebee queens to wake up! It's their job to find food and look for a suitable nest location. She then lays her eggs and can sit on them for around two weeks to keep them warm.

Monarch butterflies begin a mass migration north from Mexico in the spring. The females fly far north to lay their eggs in the southern States.

Castelluccio in the Italian mountain range of the Apennines is popular with skiers in winter. In spring, it's carpeted with beautiful seasonal blooms.

My Jaunty Blackbird

Merry Mr Blackbird
Illuminates my day,
Hopping on the lawn,
His head is turned my way!
Those brightest sparkling eyes,
That vivid yellow beak,
His jet-black shining feathers –
My favourite for his cheek!
He stops and looks around,
In charge, he cocks his head.
A robin keeps his distance;
The sparrows have all fled!
Now he pecks the ground
For a worm or other treat,
Before he spots an apple –
He loves that juice so sweet!
It's spring so Mrs Blackbird,
Her feathers sooty brown,
Is guarding in their nest
Their young in silky down.

George Hughes.

The Little Things

"Little things please little minds"
I've sometimes heard folk say,
As if the smaller things of life
Weren't worth the time of day.
Yet, surely it's the little things
That make our lives worthwhile?
A snatch of song, a lovely view,
Or just a friendly smile.
For if we treasure all the things
That drive away dull care,
They'll make our lives more truly rich
Than any millionaire!

Maggie Ingall.

45

Strawberry Moon

So round and full, his ancient face
Rises late in the darkening sky,
As down below small creatures fear
To hear the beat of wings go by.
Tender lovers' hands entwine
To make their vows within his sight,
While those who might have lost their way
Are drawn towards his guiding light.
He offers no answers, how or why,
Just smiles benignly and drifts on by.

Laura Tapper.

Summer's Swell

Summer enters on the tail feathers
Of spring, with lengthening days,
And longer spells of sunshine.

Colour dots the garden, borderlines
Of flowering shrubs, poppies,
Daisies bobbing in the breeze.

Blackbirds claim their trees,
Their territorial songs ring out
In complicated verses.

And only rain throws curses
At summer's swell; all is well
As days stretch lazily.

Heather Walker.

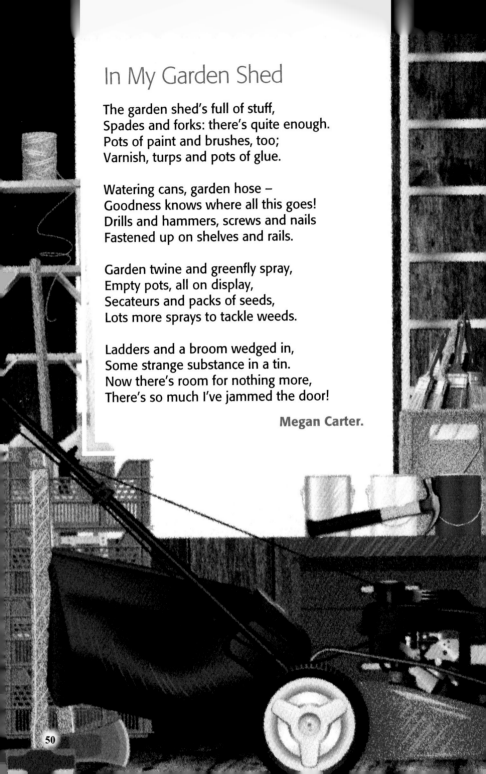

In My Garden Shed

The garden shed's full of stuff,
Spades and forks: there's quite enough.
Pots of paint and brushes, too;
Varnish, turps and pots of glue.

Watering cans, garden hose –
Goodness knows where all this goes!
Drills and hammers, screws and nails
Fastened up on shelves and rails.

Garden twine and greenfly spray,
Empty pots, all on display,
Secateurs and packs of seeds,
Lots more sprays to tackle weeds.

Ladders and a broom wedged in,
Some strange substance in a tin.
Now there's room for nothing more,
There's so much I've jammed the door!

Megan Carter.

Summer Healing

The summer brings us many gifts
With flowers, bushes, trees,
The smell of perfume in the air,
The touch of gentle breeze.
The happy sounds as children play,
Enjoying so much fun –
And we can feel more hopeful, too,
Uplifted by the sun.

Those darker days of winter
Were simply swept along,
And we can share the healing time
To make our spirits strong.
Rejoice in beauty, light and shade,
The comfort of the sun,
And open up your heart and mind –
The healing has begun!

Iris Hesselden.

Cloud Puffs

It seems as if an army
Is approaching through the air,
But the puffs of cream and white
Drift by without a care.

Their long and gentle journey
Lasts many days and nights,
They let the warm wind blow them
Over many wondrous sights.

They float above the mountains
And they sail across the seas,
They journey over desert lands,
All guided by the breeze.

And when their journey's ended,
Then they simply disappear –
A performance of pure magic
Somewhere in the atmosphere.

Lily Christie.

A Holiday Romance

Off to work, the morning commute,
A walk to the station in a smart business suit.
I stand on the platform, awaiting the train,
And, as it pulls in, it's starting to rain.
Lucky for me, today I've a seat,
Next to the window where I can retreat
Into my daydreams as rooftops race by,
Seeing, instead, what's in my mind's eye.
Fields starred with daisies on a bright sunlit day,
Where a stream ripples by, with otters at play.
I follow this stream till it reaches the sea.
There, on its beach, with cliffs behind me
I walk hand in hand with this person I've met,
A "holiday romance" that I'll never forget.
The years may have passed, but the memories stay,
Of someone who's lived in my heart every day.
And on my way home, what carries me through,
Is my "holiday romance" – whom I'm married to.

John Darley.

Summer Is Coming

WHAT makes a good summer? For me, it's Wimbledon – the highlight of my year. For two weeks I'm glued to the television (and on a number of occasions I've been lucky to get tickets in the public ballot).

It's not just the tennis I love, it's the setting: the greenery, the buildings, the buzz of people and traffic. I love sitting on Henman Hill, listening to the thwack of balls on rackets over the grounds, the clapping and roar of the crowd, umpires calling the scores.

I love looking at the London skyline to the north and the spire of St Mary's church to the south. I love late evenings on an outside court with shadows lengthening across the grass.

When Wimbledon is on, then all is well with the world.

It begins with the anticipation of the tournament at the start of the spring. I think of all that lies ahead and feel joy in my heart.

What will the draw look like?

What stories will unfold over the fortnight? Who will triumph?

It's all to look forward to. Whatever your thing is, don't we all feel joy as summer approaches?

The good news is, when it comes to the kingdom of God, it's all about summer and we can anticipate it with joy.

Even though there may be tears at night, as the psalmist says, joy comes in the morning.

Through the dark days of winter, we know that summer is going to come again and that sustains us; we know that joy lies ahead.

The writer of the letter to the Hebrews says, "Let us fix our eyes on Jesus, the author and perfector of our faith, who for the joy set before him endured the cross, scorning its shame, and sat down at the right hand of the throne of God."

Jesus's whole ministry could have been overshadowed by the knowledge that the cross lay ahead, yet when we look at his life, we realise that this

Shutterstock.

by Rev. Susan Sarapuk

▶ was far from the case.

We read about him being filled with joy when his disciples came back from a mission and reported that people were healed and delivered. Jesus wants the joy he has to be in his disciples.

Anybody who enjoyed parties and dinners, who every day saw people dancing and rejoicing because they'd been healed or delivered, could not be as dour and as serious as some people paint him to be.

There were tough times, but I have the feeling that belonging to that band of disciples and travelling with Jesus must have been an incredible, joyous summer experience.

The kingdom of God is like summer. Jesus compares the kingdom to a wedding banquet. Now, who's sad at a wedding?

It's no mistake that C.S. Lewis entitles his biography "Surprised By Joy". That is who God is – he is joy.

When we finally understand, it's like being overwhelmed with joy, a recognition of something we knew all along: a coming home.

Even before we encounter God, we experience stirrings within us, a sense of joy: the sight of a sunset, standing at the edge of the ocean, being on top of a mountain.

Every person catches that feeling in their hearts from time to time and feels there must be more.

C.S. Lewis writes, "No soul that seriously and constantly desires joy will ever miss it. Those who seek find. To those who knock it is opened."

God speaks this promise through his prophet: "You will seek me and find me when you seek me with all of your heart."

There is a time of seeking and a time of waiting, but there's no doubt about the joy ahead.

When I'm wrapped up against the wind and rain in the depths of winter, I think of sunny days wearing T-shirts and shorts, walking the dog along the river in dappled shade.

I think of the Chelsea Flower Show, Wimbledon, trips to the seaside and outdoor concerts.

And so, in the kingdom of God, it will be summer, however dreary and difficult things seem now, and nothing will be able to stop its arrival. Indeed, it's already begun.

The kingdom of God breaks into our lives where people are healed and delivered today, where there is goodness and kindness.

Even when evil appears to triumph in a fallen world, we know that God will wipe away every tear and right every wrong.

C.S. Lewis writes about this.

"Either the day must come when joy prevails and all makers of misery are no longer able to infect it: or else for ever and ever the makers of misery can destroy in others the happiness they reject for themselves."

January is the worst month of

the year. It's a long time until spring, and summer seems like a forgotten country. Yet, in the tennis calendar, it's the month of the Australian Open.

I feel that sense of joy, knowing it's starting again – the American hard court season, the clay court season, the French Open, the grass court season culminating in Wimbledon. It's all ahead!

When it's grey and dark, I know that Wimbledon is getting nearer with every day. Summer is coming and nothing can stop it. Thus it is with the kingdom of God, our summer place of joy for ever.

Wait for it, anticipate it, play your part in working for it. Joy is coming – it cannot fail. ■

Nature's Calendar For Summer

Real hummingbirds are only found in the Americas, but in the UK we can see hummingbird hawk-moths. They hover just like their namesakes, but their tongues extend to the flowers, not their bills.

Whilst fox cubs are normally born in March, they're the right age in early summer to be out and about playing together.

During the summer, around 1,800 thunderstorms are occurring at any given time! Most thunderstorms go on for around 30 minutes and are typically about 15 miles in diameter.

Shutterstock.

If you spot a baby bird on the ground, it might be there on purpose. Some spend time on the ground building their strength as they learn to fly at this time of year. The parents are probably nearby, so it's best left alone.

It's the perfect time to visit Oze National Park in Japan. This stunning place boasts an enormous marsh area surrounded by mountains. There are walks across the marshes on miles of wooden boardwalk.

Stinging nettles might not be your favourite plant to share the garden with, but they're great for butterflies. A number of species, including red admirals and comma butterfly caterpillars, dine on the leaves in summer.

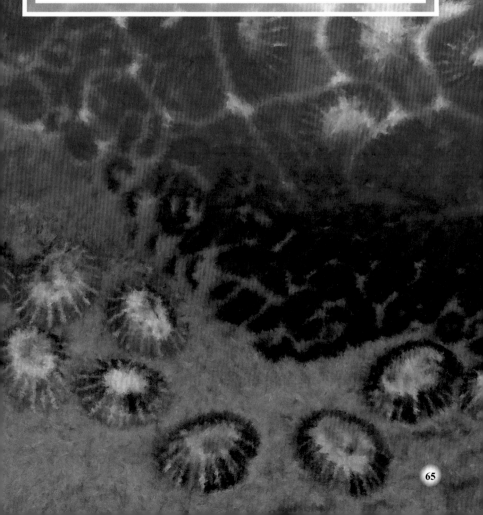

Seashells

A walk along a seashore reveals a thousand jewels.
They lie among the shingle, they hide in rocky pools.
They shine from 'neath the water, small sculptures, each unique,
Some marked by tide and tempest, some perfect, satin sleek.
Smooth silver-blue of mussels, and periwinkles, bright,
Carved cockleshells and limpets, each one a small delight.
Each one a tiny artwork, a gift from nature's store,
So stop and look; enjoy them, these treasures from the shore.

Maggie Ingall.

A Day In The Hills

As I crested a hill and I looked to the north,
I was drawn to the fabulous view.
So how to resist the strong urge to set forth
And to sample adventures anew?

I descended the slope, in the midsummer heat,
To be met by the cool of the trees.
And I warily chose where I planted my feet,
While the squirrels cavorted with ease.

I emerged from the wood, to the heat of the day,
Where the river flowed slowly along.
There were pollarded willows to show me the way,
And the birds filled the air with their song.

I've been out here all day, gaily wandering free,
And should soon bring my walk to an end.
It's past time for tea, but I'm eager to see
Just what's waiting around the next bend . . .

Dennis W. Turner.

A Sea Mist

A perfect, sparkling summer's day,
With sand and sea an endless view,
And air like wine; the cloudless sky
A glorious, optimistic blue.
The shell-strewn rocks are hot to touch,
Gulls swoop and soar above the sea,
Their cries are harsh and jubilant
Because they're flying wild and free.
The clear horizon starts to fade –
A gauzy mist is gathering there
And fills and thickens, moving fast,
The taste of salt is in the air.
This blanket moves relentlessly
Obliterating sea and sky;
The world is now a lonely grey,
The unseen gulls no longer cry.

Eileen Hay.

Discovered

Lost along a shaded path,
Taken by mistake,
The timid cottage hides and seems
To hardly be awake.

Its leaded lattice windows peer
Between the plants which climb:
Wisteria, a rambling rose,
Clematis all entwined.

A heavy scent of herb and bloom
Is carried on the breeze.
There's naught to hear but songs of birds,
The lazy hum of bees.

As I lean upon the gate,
All sense of time has gone,
I'll leave the cottage there in peace,
That it may slumber on.

Laura Tapper.

Rooftop Retreat

Gazing to the misty line
Where ocean meets the sky,
Pondering and dreaming dreams
As time ticks slowly by.

I've the perfect vantage point,
A calm, rooftop retreat,
Watching white-sailed yachts drift by,
Contentment is complete.

Tomorrow, when the world pounds in
And I've somewhere else to be,
This day will dance in memory,
Like sunbeams on the sea.

Marian Cleworth.

Buttercups

Buttercups are everywhere,
Scattered through the fields,
Yellow faces upward turned,
Shy beauty is revealed.
Gleaming through the blades of grass,
Like little suns they shine,
Their petals soft and delicate,
Their shimmering divine.
Like bright confetti on the ground,
It's summer's celebration,
Of lazy days and starry nights,
And nature's ostentation.

Lily Christie.

Wish You Were Here?

Collecting postcards is good fun,
Not only for the views.
If there is writing on the back,
Those are the ones I'll choose.

Arrived in sun but rain today;
Our landlady is grumpy:
She boiled Ken's egg for far too long;
Maud says her bed is lumpy.

Dear Mum and Dad, forgive us, please.
(First class from Gretna Green!)
We are in love, and not too young –
We're nearly seventeen!

I have some sent from battlefields;
This one is from the Somme.
My darling Lil, when I come home,
Please marry me, love, Tom.

I'd love to know, did Mum and Dad
Forgive those newlyweds?
Did Maud enjoy her holiday,
Despite that lumpy bed?

But most of all I pray that Tom
Was spared to marry Lil,
And they sent their own postcards, too,
From Blackpool, Rye and Rhyl.

Kathryn Sennen.

Wish you were here

Greetings from Blackpool

BLACKPOO

KISS ME QUICK

ACH
LAN
S QUIC

EEN

SCOTLAND
By Train

CARTE POSTALE

Slàinte
Mhath!

BONNIE
SCOTLAND

77

Making Memories

A LL in all, it was a never-to-be-forgotten summer – one of those summers which come seldom into any life, but leave a rich heritage of beautiful memories in their going.

"One of those summers which, in a fortunate combination of delightful weather, delightful friends and delightful doings, come as near to perfection as anything can come in this world."

I'm choosing to remind you of those words, not just because I love L.M. Montgomery's "Anne Of Green Gables" books, but also because they seem to encapsulate all our hopes and expectations for this kindest of seasons.

For we always do seem to approach summer with the highest of hopes. Almost as soon as the last Easter egg has been eaten, we see shop windows start to sport mannequins wearing the latest swimwear, sandals and designer sunglasses.

Advertisements appear, urging us not to forget to buy our sun-screen and travel toiletries, while garden centres offer not only a range of summer bedding plants, but garden swings and parasols, and top-of-the-range barbecue equipment.

Even if we can resist the temptation to rush out and buy, they all go to feed our dreams. We see them and imagine days of blue skies and sunshine, happy hours spent lazing on beaches or in flower-filled meadows.

We visualise picnics, ice-creams and long convivial evenings in the garden, laughing and talking until the first stars appear in the sky.

Except, of course, it isn't always like that. Sometimes those long-anticipated days of sunshine, leisure and exploring new places simply fail to materialise.

Sometimes we have weeks where the weather is too chilly to sit on a beach wearing those latest fashions.

Sometimes, more rarely, it's too hot, and gardeners are forced to watch their much-prized

by Maggie Ingall

▶ gardens suffering from drought. Sometimes the pollen count makes life a misery for hay fever victims. Sometimes holidays get cancelled, or just never work out quite as well as we hoped they would.

Take Richard and Sally, for example. Together with two friends, they had booked their Mediterranean cruise months beforehand.

They set off with new cases, new clothes and much excitement, and within a few days we received a stream of e-mails showing all the places they were visiting – although not, we noticed, with much accompanying information as to how they were enjoying it.

"It was nothing like as good as I'd imagined it would be," Sally reported disconsolately when I bumped into her a day or two after their return.

"None of the destinations proved to be as interesting as we'd anticipated. Our cabin wasn't perfect, nor was the food. And we had two whole afternoons when it rained. I'd been expecting sunshine every day!"

I had to suppress a small smile, I must admit. It would indeed be wonderful if all holidays – and life itself! – could be sunshine every day.

Yet when I later happened to meet the friends with whom they had travelled, it seemed a different story.

They had enjoyed all the places they'd visited, and been perfectly happy with both the food and with their accommodation.

Which just went to show, I felt, that both happiness and disappointment can be found wherever we happen to search for them.

I often feel that my aunt Dora is a good example of that attitude. She'd always been an adventurous traveller, but as the years went by she found herself swapping exotic far-flung destinations for the more sedate pleasures of domestic coach holidays.

Knowing her to be staying in a West Country seaside resort during 10 days of particularly heavy rain, I was not optimistic as to her chances of having enjoyed her time away.

I need not have worried. When I called in on her return, she greeted me with a pot of tea and a beaming smile.

"Have one of these Cornish cream cookies," she urged. "They served these at the hotel, and when I told the waitress just how much I liked them, they gave me a bag to take home with me!"

I laughed. Aunt Dora has always had a knack of making friends with those around her, and of finding the local people just as interesting as the places she visits.

"But what about the weather?" I pressed. "I imagine the rain must have put a damper on lots of things, in more ways than one."

"Well, perhaps a little," she

admitted. "It wasn't possible to amble round the town very much, nor sit on a harbour bench and watch the boats. But the hotel had an excellent supply of books, jigsaws and board games, so there was always plenty to do.

"Do you know," she added, "I hadn't done a jigsaw since I was a child? But I noticed that there was rather a nice one on the shelf, so I thought I might as well have a go.

"After a while, another lady came and joined me, then a family with two children, and before long there were several of us all trying to fit pieces. It's amazing how good a large jigsaw can be at breaking the ice!

"Soon we were chatting together about all sorts of things, and the time just flew by. I may not have a suntan from my holiday, but I certainly made some new friends."

Thank goodness for people like Aunt Dora. By looking for the positives in any situation she invariably finds them.

Which rather helpfully leads me to share another favourite quote from "Anne Of Green Gables".

"It's been my experience that you can nearly always enjoy things if you make up your mind firmly that you will."

That proves to me that it isn't the weather, or the location, that can make the difference between a good summer and a bad one – it's how we choose to view it! ∎

Nature's Calendar For Summer

The cactus mouse avoids the heat of desert days, seeking refuge in crevices. It stays still in the day, lowering its heart rate so it doesn't need food or water, then feeds after sunset.

If you are in Antarctica as winter descends, you're stuck until summer comes around. Conditions are too treacherous for travel, but it's a great time for astronomers, who benefit from the complete, deep darkness and crisp, clear skies.

The sound of grasshoppers isn't as common as it used to be, but if you're lucky you might still hear their soft "chirping". Both male and female grasshoppers can produce the sound, but it's usually the males making it as they search for a mate.

Shutterstock.

The beautiful bumblebee orchid grows in warm countries like Turkey and the Canary Islands. Its shape bears an uncanny resemblance to a lady bee, which attracts the male bumblebees for polllination.

You might have to wait longer for dark skies in late summer, but August is the perfect time for stargazing. The Perseids meteor shower is one of the most spectacular sights in the night sky, and it's at its best in August.

Cloudberries are much like raspberries or blackberries, but are one of the few fruits native to the Arctic. Picking them in season is a common activity in Scandinavian countries, and they're delicious made into jam.

A Different World

Grandad and Gran worked together,
On their croft in the far Hebrides;
An island so small, with few people,
Where front doors had no need of keys.

In the summer I'd go with my parents,
Enjoying a long holiday.
That thrill as the ferry drew nearer,
And the taste of the salty sea spray.

On their island, time had no purpose,
The seasons and weather meant more;
Folk lived and they worked without question,
As their ancestors had done so before.

When I look back, I mostly remember
How contentment shone out from each face:
Grandad, with pipe, making hurdles,
And Gran with her bobbins and lace.

Today, when life appears hectic,
I'll pause and recall those lost days
With Grandad and Gran on their island
And the light from the sun's setting rays.

John Darley.

Farmyard Swallows

When the doors are left wide open
In our barn on summer days,
The yearly plight of swallows
Never ceases to amaze.
In the gable ends are windows,
Where they flutter all the day,
Although we try to help them,
To escape the easy way.

To fly downwards seems so easy
To us – but not to them;
So we leave the large doors open
In the evenings now and then.
The fading light attracts them
When it's darker there inside:
A helpful easier option
For them to use as a guide.

Yet what a strange anomaly,
It always seems to me,
To fly so many thousand miles
Across both land and sea,
Then insist on entering a barn
From which they can't get out;
It's a subject farmers question
Each year, there is no doubt.

Dawn Lawrence.

Ken's Bench

My father built his own garden bench,
Using solid, sustainable wood.
And with his skill, and his carpentry tools,
Made something that looked really good.

For years it stood under an apple tree,
Where he'd see how his garden had thrived,
From the efforts he'd made bringing life to the soil,
As, above him, the swallows arrived.

In summer, quite often, I'd join him,
As he paused from his work for a rest.
Together we'd sit on the bench that he'd made
Whilst the swallows fed young in the nest.

His bench has now moved to my garden,
But the memory of Ken will live on.
For, when I sit on it, I still feel him near,
Long after the swallows have gone.

John Darley.

Autumn

He arrives in a coat of many colours:
Flame, gold, russet and brown.
Autumn appears with dancing feet,
Crunching on leaves the wind has blown down.

Rustling and bustling, friend with the wind,
Whistling and blowing and whooshing around,
Creating a carpet of multiple colours,
Teasing the leaves as they fall to the ground.

Mellowing fruits and ripening corn,
Autumn's bounty for us to share,
The days will shorten, it's time to rest –
As seasons change and winter draws near.

Megan Carter.

A Small Miracle!

An early childhood memory
Is walking with my dad,
Just me, without big sister –
(And that fact made me glad!)
He picked up a large conker,
Still in its coat of green,
And said, "We'll now see something
The world has never seen!"
He split the spiky casing
And there, to my delight,
I saw this shiny object
Like wood that's polished bright!
Then several decades later,
My small grandson and I
Walked under a horse chestnut
And something caught my eye –
A spiky round green conker.
I held it in my hand;
"We'll now see something special
Seen by no-one in the land!"

Eileen Hay.

92

Reading With Toby

"Don't like books, miss!" Toby moans
And sits down with a sigh.
"I've brought you different ones," I say.
"Maybe just give one a try?"

He glances at the covers,
His interest, he can't hide.
"I like the pictures, miss," he says,
And slowly looks inside.

We start off very gently
Till his confidence takes flight,
And soon we've finished one whole page
To Toby's great delight.

He sounds each word out carefully
And listens to advice.
The story makes him laugh out loud
So he wants to read it twice.

When I suggest he takes one home,
Toby smiles and whispers, "Wow!
Can we read again tomorrow, miss?
'Cause I think I like books now!"

Kate Bradbury.

Song Of The Harvest

Decked out in its finest, the country church stands
Amongst the fields of livestock and acres of land
Where crops have been grown for generations before.
Now all good folk gather for harvest once more.
The display on the table shows nature's great bounty
Of fruits, grains and vegetables grown in this county.
Chestnuts in prickly pompoms reside,
The harvest loaf placed in the centre with pride,
Donations of packets and tins brought to share
With people in need, to show that we care.
So now join our voices to joyfully sing
Of all the great blessings that harvest-time brings.

Laura Tapper.

The Otter

In a furrow of bubbles once –
He became –
The ever-flowing curve of a thing
That can never be still,
From the first stirrings of pink
When morning lies in the window of the east
Like a new-caught salmon, he's off:
Sewn out of rivers and hills, a bend of grace –
His nose telling ten thousand tales,
Everything listening inside, eager
To be under and over and through
This element he can never let go –
Born out of water,
Water made otter.

Kenneth Steven.

A Time Of Renewal

WE had three generations of the family together and my daughter-in-law had a new camera. It was too good a chance to waste. We piled into the cars and headed for the park.

The park – once the gardens of a stately home – had lots of old established trees, and the leaves would be every colour from wine-red to banana-yellow to burnished copper.

There would be enough on the ground for the children to play in and enough still on the trees to make stunning backdrops for family portraits.

Autumn seems to be a time of innocence, doesn't it?

The children rolled down hills into banked piles of leaves without caring what else might be in them. Their parents tried to keep the little ones safe without spoiling their fun.

Someone suggested there might be hedgehogs in some of the piles. The noise level went down as the younger ones went burrowing – but quietly, so as not to wake the hedgehogs.

Two of the older cousins ran as fast as they could around a tree, apparently trying to create a whirlwind that would blow more leaves up into the air.

Leaf-angels were attempted. They mostly failed, but what child doesn't delight in lying on a bed of leaves and waving their arms and legs about?

Soon it was time to round everyone up, keeping smiles on their faces, for the family portraits.

Daughter-in-law had her camera on the stand and was setting the timer when the first drop of rain fell on the back of her hand.

Uh-oh! A few drops quickly turned into a downpour. Babies were popped into prams, walking-poles and footballs were gathered, and everyone in the park dashed for the car park.

The park ranger was lifting a raincoat from his vehicle as we were tumbling into ours.

"The weather is so ▶

by David McLaughlan

unpredictable," I complained.

"Not if you look at the weather report," he said.

I conceded his point and we laughed. He asked what we'd been up to and I told him about our attempted photo shoot.

"Why don't you come back the day after tomorrow?" he asked. "It's to be dry then. This rain will have given the trees a real boost. It'll be worth it!"

We had a family meeting and decided we could make it happen. Some might have agreed just because daughter-in-law looked so disappointed.

I don't think anyone gave much credence to the ranger's words. At best, they probably thought he'd just checked the weather report.

So we returned.

The difference was dramatic: the yellows were more golden, the browns looked more polished, the reds had a sparkle.

The whole park seemed more alive. Even the smiles on our faces seemed brighter, as if they were saying, "We did it! This time!"

Daughter-in-law agreed her camera had taken some fine pictures, but there was more to it.

"We could have had an ordinary day," she said. "Instead we had a wash-out of a day. And that gave us a better day!"

What we saw as a "wash-out day" was, for the trees and bushes in the park, a time of renewal.

And then I spoiled it by taking everyone out for dinner.

Why do I say that? I was thinking about renewal – and fasting! Mention fasting to most people and they think of days without food. A good meal out is the opposite of that.

Actually, fasting isn't really about not eating. Meals are just another distraction to be set aside during daylight hours. The real focus of a fast is renewing your relationship with God!

All through the Bible people go through difficult times – wash-out days, if you like – to be renewed. Mostly, they are involuntary. But those in the know used them for a purpose.

Saul spent his days of blindness in prayer, reappraising his understanding of God.

Esther fasted for three days and prayed for the courage to ask King Xerxes to spare the Jewish people.

After his baptism, Jesus fasted for 40 days and 40 nights. Why? Because this man the world had never heard of was about to change everything.

It was never about the food for them. It was about renewing their relationship with the Almighty. Those would have been difficult times – wash-out days – but each one of them emerged better for the experience.

Renewal is a regular part of life. Autumn exists because summer did its work, then stepped aside until the next year.

Leaves fall and feed the soil for new trees to grow.

Friends were making a mess of their marriage, until they renewed their vows and started over again with a new focus on what they loved about each other.

As sad a thought as it may be for the younger folks, grandchildren and great-grandchildren will renew the family when I step aside. God and I have talked about that – and we wouldn't have it any other way.

Until then, I'll be a phone and video-call grandad when they are all at their separate homes, preparing to turn into the best grandad ever whenever we manage to get together.

Of course, most of us don't take the wash-out days or the fasting days and the changes they bring easily. We are creatures of habit, and habit isn't growth.

But we might get into the habit of setting time aside to reconnect with God, listen to him and emerge better for it.

A Sabbath of your own, say. Perhaps even with meals. But definitely with a purpose.

And if some of those times are also spent with family, reconnect with what they are all about, remind them where they come from and give them the strength to go where they need to go.

My youngest granddaughter's wellies had three red and green leaves stuck to them.

They're in front of me now. I'm going to return those leaves to the park. They still have some renewing to do. ■

Nature's Calendar For *Autumn*

Snails eat mushrooms and fungi, but in autumn they're just as likely to climb up on to them to catch the last of the year's warm rays.

Murmurations of starlings are a familiar sight in northern Europe, but in Denmark they call the phenomenon a "black sun". Huge numbers of them gather at the Wadden Sea National Park's marshlands.

Lake Bled in Slovenia is a particularly stunning place to enjoy the autumn colours. It's a tourist trap in the summer, but September and October are calm for visitors, and the trees look beautiful, set off by the mountainous backdrop.

Wolves are known for their characteristic howl, but not all howls are the same. Each wolf has its own howl, which helps identify other members of the pack when not together.

Spiders often spin their webs at night during autumn, giving them time to make them larger to catch food as the pickings get slim. Cool, dewy mornings cover them in droplets, making them a spectacular sight in the mornings.

In Greek mythology, autumn began when Demeter – the goddess of the harvest – reacted to her daughter Persephone's abduction by causing all the crops on earth to die. Spring marks the time Persephone was released and allowed to return.

Out Of This World

"Gran can make a planet!"
That really is not true.
Perhaps a model version?
Papier-mâché will do.

"Gran can make an astronaut;
Send him to the moon."
Not true, but with this cloth scrap
We can dress a wooden spoon.

"Gran can make a rocket ship,
To blast off into space."
We will take these empty boxes,
Tape them neatly into place.

The spaceman's in his rocket:
Count backwards, down from three.
No need for fuel or rocket gas –
Imagination, that's the key!

Angie Keeler.

A Woodland Walk

Entering the woods, I take the path that leads me through,
Beneath the oaks and sycamores, past elder, birch and yew.
I love this peaceful place – I'm thankful for so many reasons:
Its kindly shade; its steadfast trees that change to mark the
  seasons.
The colours of their vibrant leaves; the haven they provide
To birds and other creatures who creep in to dwell or hide.
For picnics held beneath them in the warmth of summertime,
When children's laughter fills the air as, joyfully, they climb.
For hours of dreamy walking – my beloved dog and I;
For trees that offer shelter when the rainclouds fill the sky.
But most of all I'm thankful for the care and dedication
Of those who thought to plant them for a future generation.

Emma Canning.

The Future Passed . . .

I was standing in my garden
Beneath the darkening sky,
Hoping for a chance to see
The space station orbit by.

And as I stood there waiting
In the stillness of the night,
A bat, a silent silhouette,
Appeared in reckless flight.

Stars now shone more brightly
As did the crescent moon.
A part of me dwelt in the past
Despite what would come soon.

And then, just like a star itself,
Its route both fixed and curved,
The ISS flew over me
As the bat still dipped and swerved.

Whilst mankind, in a spacecraft,
New frontiers still explores,
The bat lives on, unchanging,
From the time of dinosaurs.

John Darley.

A Little Note To Self . . .

There's something I need to remember
Though it's not what I firmly believe.
'Cause I've lived all my life with the motto
That's it's better to give than receive.

It's a principle that doesn't fail me –
Choosing "giving" will never be wrong –
But I'm sometimes at risk of forgetting
I can't run on near-empty for long.

By the evening there's so little time left
To put into feeling restored –
So why wait till after the work's done?
Receiving's not just a reward!

So tomorrow, if I need some "me-time",
Be it book, meditation or rest,
I shall start the day off by receiving –
And begin it by feeling my best!

Emma Canning.

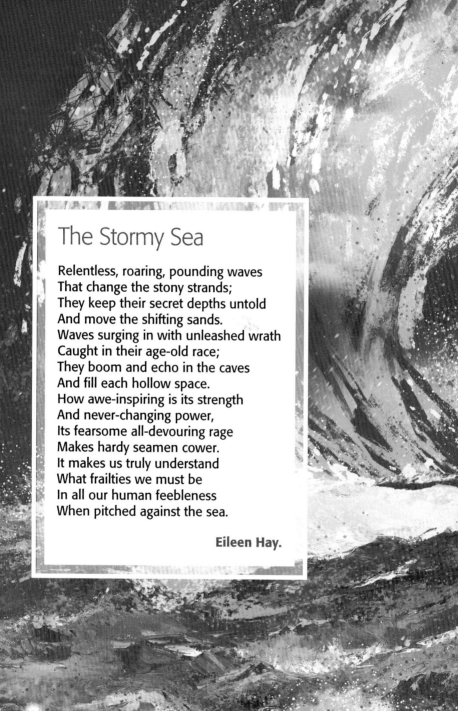

The Stormy Sea

Relentless, roaring, pounding waves
That change the stony strands;
They keep their secret depths untold
And move the shifting sands.
Waves surging in with unleashed wrath
Caught in their age-old race;
They boom and echo in the caves
And fill each hollow space.
How awe-inspiring is its strength
And never-changing power,
Its fearsome all-devouring rage
Makes hardy seamen cower.
It makes us truly understand
What frailties we must be
In all our human feebleness
When pitched against the sea.

Eileen Hay.

"For Sale"

If ever I am travelling, and I see a house for sale,
Especially if it's empty, then I ponder on its tale.
For what could be the reason that its owners went away?
Is it crumbling? Is it haunted? Is it noisy night and day?
Did the owners win a fortune? Have they bought a posher place?
Or are they having triplets, and they need the extra space?
Have they gone to join a circus? Have they left for far Mumbai?
Retired to the country, just to watch the world go by?
There's one thing that is certain, though I'm sad to say it's so,
Whatever is the reason, I'm afraid I'll never know!

Maggie Ingall.

FOR SALE

INN

B & B

for sale

for sale

19

FOR SALE

FOR SALE

117

Precious Patchwork

My quilt is multi-coloured and it's taken years to grow,
Though it is far from perfect, it has been a joy to sew.
Some of the squares are tiny, just little scraps to spare,
Yet each holds special meaning and is crafted with great care.
A dress my daughter treasured, a tablecloth – long frayed,
A bedspread scrap from childhood I cannot bear let fade.
These are my fabric relics that rekindle days now past
So rich with many blessings for a new quilt stitched to last.
This is my special memory quilt which is no task to do,
Bringing memories back to life to live again anew.

Judy Jarvie.

from the Manse Window

Autumn Promises

I RECALL a film version of "Tess Of The D'Urbervilles" from the early 1980s. To be more precise, I recall a small part of it.

The composition of the scene was so stunning that the image has stayed with me.

Angel Clare, played by Peter Finch, was standing in the middle of an autumn woodland, and all around him golden leaves fell like snow from the trees. It was simply breathtaking.

I remember nothing else of the film.

I love the smells and the colours of autumn.

Pinned on the noticeboards in my study, along with records of my writing work, quotes from the Bible and pieces of information I need easy access to, are a number of pictures I've cut out from magazines, the majority of which depict the woodland in autumn.

Have you noticed how the most vibrant colours put in an appearance right at the very end of the season, usually in the first week of November?

There's a copse of oak trees near to where I live where the indifferent coppers and browns suddenly glow gold at this time.

In my garden the acer flames crimson and the ornamental cherry is a blaze of orange and red.

By the end of autumn the flounce and flourish of summer days are long gone, the harvest is over and the land is preparing for hibernation.

Yet, while everything is going quiet, shedding and dying, we know that underneath the ground something is still going on, preparing for the spring that lies not too far in the future.

We plant tulips in November, aware that we won't see the results until late spring, trusting that something is going on deep in the earth.

We have different seasons in our lives and different seasons in our walk of faith, too.

When everything seems to be shutting down, there are

Shutterstock.

---

by Rev. Susan Sarapuk

still things going on – even though we might not be aware of it. In the fallow times we are building up our future growth.

Years ago, when I was a young Christian, our local church life was very exciting. On my return from university, where I'd had a conversion experience, I'd met up with a group of others who were on the same wavelength as me.

We held a weekly Bible study, we formed a worship group, we were in and out of each other's houses, encouraging one another, praising the Lord, praying together.

We were full of plans for moving in together, starting a community and opening a book shop and coffee shop. We had a vicar who was open to new things. We were waiting for a glorious harvest.

None of the plans materialised.

The vicar moved on and his replacement was suspicious, rather than open. One by one my friends were selected to train for ministry and moved away.

I was unemployed and drifting, wondering what to do with my life once I realised I didn't want to teach, which is what I'd trained for.

It was a very fallow time in contrast to the previous times of joy and promise and the expectation of a rich harvest.

Yet things were happening beneath the surface. God was calling us to different things even though we'd wanted to stay together. He had different plans

for us. Although the dying was painful, it had to happen.

Eventually, I, too, was called to train for ordination.

The good thing is that we are all still friends today, despite spending our working lives in different places.

We need the fallow times, the autumn season, in order to move into the next spurt of growth in our spiritual lives.

It's easy to be stuck in our ways because it's comfortable. In the fallow times we have a chance to go deeper, to build a relationship with God without distractions.

I think this was particularly true during the spring and early summer in 2020 when we couldn't go to church.

Did you give up because you couldn't go to church?

Christians are meant to gather together because we are the body of Christ. Communion, liturgy, singing, preaching, praying together, fellowship – all these are part of our worship, but when they're stripped away, what do we have left? Is church-going sometimes a substitute for that one-to-one relationship with God?

Paul writes with a passion: "I want to know Christ and the power of his resurrection, and the fellowship of sharing in his sufferings, becoming like him in his death."

That desire drove him on.

As he wrote these words he was imprisoned in Rome. He must

Shutterstock

have been itching to get back out there, sharing the gospel, planting churches, encouraging the established ones.

Yet, in his autumn season, Paul knew that God was at work in him. Just because he was confined and prevented from doing the work he loved, it didn't mean the end of things.

Whatever is going on in our lives – anxiety, uncertainty, a season of shedding and dying – the best thing we can do is always to look to God, to spend time in his presence, because we can be sure that, even in the fallow times, when all seems to be coming to an end, he is at work deep within us, preparing us for what is to come.

Jesus said to seek first the kingdom of God and everything we need would be ours. He promised to be with us always, that he would never let us go, and he said that he wanted us to be fruitful.

God is not done with us, even in the autumn season. ■

Nature's Calendar For *Autumn*

Longer and cooler nights make fog more likely during the autumn months than in summer. The fog usually develops overnight and hangs around until the temperature builds up during the day.

With hibernation on the way, bears need to stock up fat reserves for winter – a process called hyperphagia. Their increased activity also makes it a good time to spot them out and about.

Ladybirds gathering in numbers was often thought to be a sign of a harsh winter on the way, but it's just what they do as the seasons change. A warm autumn day might see groups of them on the sunny side of your house or garden as they soak up the warmth.

Limes do actually turn yellow like their lemon cousins when they're fully ripe and rich with fruit sugars, but they're hard to keep in this condition so tend to be shipped around the world whilst in their green, under-ripe state.

It's common to think "fall" is the American version of "autumn", but "fall" was actually common in England in the 17th century. It changed in Britain in the 18th century after the French *l'automne*, but American migrants kept the original phrase.

It's not uncommon for Canada and Alaska to see snowfall while the rest of the northern hemisphere is still enjoying autumn. Canada's snowiest place is Woody Point on the coast of Newfoundland. It typically gets around 6.38 metres or 21 feet of snow over just three months.

The Silvery Moon

Slipping from the midnight cloud
A silver bowl streaked Wedgwood blue
Strokes the river, fingers through
The wind-blown ice-cold rivulets.

Clouds skirt over, hide from view
Her capture in this watery place,
A mirror image of her face
Before she slides away.

Then, once again, a tear appears
Across the wall of night-time sky,
She's slowly peeping, photo-shy,
Unconscious of her beauty.

Heather Walker.

From The Sky

She always opened a window,
Whatever time of the year,
And looked to see what the day might bring,
If the sky was dark or clear.

She left it loose upon the latch,
Then threw it open wide,
In the hope a leaf or flower head
Might find its way inside.

A feather may have floated down;
A moth that fluttered by;
Some tiny gift might come to her
That drifted from the sky.

It might be a swirling snowflake
In the hardest winter of all,
Or the lonely cry of a sea bird,
Or maybe nothing at all.

She drew her warmth and strength from this,
A simple daily deed
That just became a habit,
And soon became a need.

It was more than just an impulse,
A sudden urge or whim;
She would always open a window
So hope could enter in.

Dawn Lawrence.

Late Autumn

Days are getting shorter;
Nights are growing cold.
The landscape in the dying light
Is turned a burnished gold.
There's stillness and there's beauty
At autumn's final phase,
Its colours now like embers,
Coated by a frosty glaze.

John Darley.

Winter Wonderland!

I've walked the seasons through the years,
Each one brings fresh delight.
The lush green spring, the surge of life,
That feels so new and bright.

Then summer with its glorious blooms,
And air so warm and sweet;
Then blazing autumn when the leaves
Form carpets at our feet.

But somehow winter beats them all,
When all the land turns white,
And sun reflecting on the snow
Bejewels everything with light!

That utter stillness in the air –
The frozen trees, the quilt of snow.
Nights so clear the midnight sky
Shines bright with starlight's glow!

Eileen Hay.

Feed The Birds

I feed the birds that visit my small garden on their way.
With peanuts, and with fat balls, I encourage them to stay.
I leave a bowl of water; they drink and bathe and play,
And have fun with each other, in a most delightful way.
It cheers me up to watch them, and wonder as I stand
How many fledglings have they fed? Do they like this helping hand?
So I'll continue feeding, stocking up their favourite snack,
Enjoying my small feathered friends – enchanted they come back!

Judy Jarvie.

135

Second-hand Home

As the sky grows velvet dark
You heave a weary sigh,
With creaking boards and knocking pipes,
You close your shuttered eyes.

Our brood has all been gathered in;
The doors locked, safe and sound.
Milk is drunk and teeth are brushed,
Alarm clocks duly wound.

Many souls across the years
Have called these four walls home;
The memories of them linger still,
Although they've long moved on.

Each family sought to make its mark
By adding something new,
But you have naught to fear from us –
We'll mould ourselves to you.

Our hearts are glad for all the love
Which feathers this old nest,
For at the close of every day –
Home, sweet home is best.

Laura Tapper.

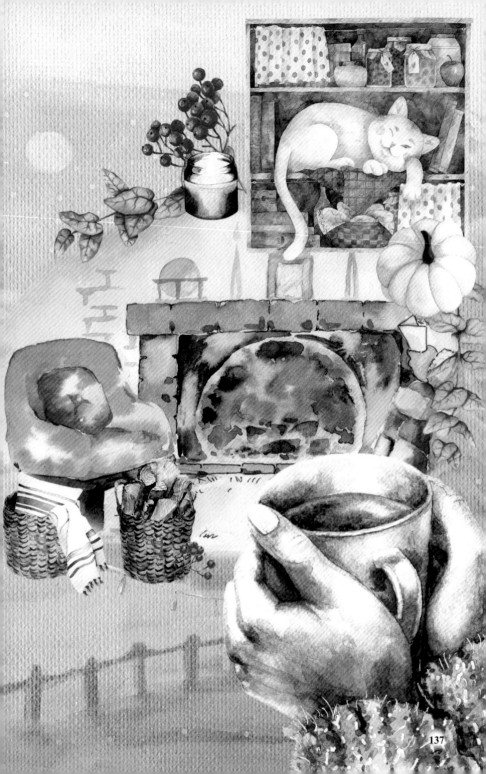

137

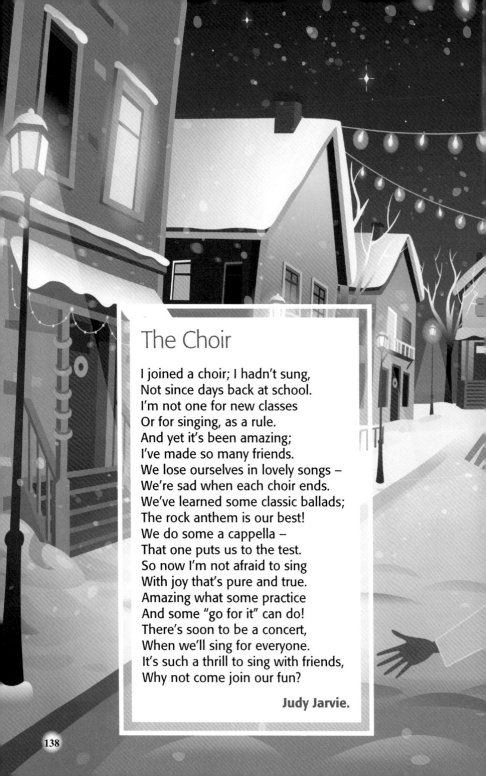

The Choir

I joined a choir; I hadn't sung,
Not since days back at school.
I'm not one for new classes
Or for singing, as a rule.
And yet it's been amazing;
I've made so many friends.
We lose ourselves in lovely songs –
We're sad when each choir ends.
We've learned some classic ballads;
The rock anthem is our best!
We do some a cappella –
That one puts us to the test.
So now I'm not afraid to sing
With joy that's pure and true.
Amazing what some practice
And some "go for it" can do!
There's soon to be a concert,
When we'll sing for everyone.
It's such a thrill to sing with friends,
Why not come join our fun?

Judy Jarvie.

The Robin

There you are, my little friend!
I know just what you need.
Come closer, ever closer,
While from my hand you feed.
At first you kept your distance,
But slowly you grew bold,
And took the crumbs of bread and cheese,
To fight the winter's cold.
Your tiny eye shines brightly –
I see your red breast swell.
Magician of the feathered world,
You have me in your spell.
You trust me not to harm you,
I'm proud to be your mate.
Same time again tomorrow?
That's settled. It's a date!

Dave Dutton.

from the Manse Window

Get Ready For Advent!

I REMEMBER vividly, early one December, trying to explain to the boys and girls in church the concept and meaning of Advent.

"If I said to you, boys and girls, that Advent, as we look towards Christmas a few weeks ahead, really just means 'arriving' or 'coming', does this help you to understand what it's all about?

"Who is coming at Christmas?" I concluded.

Well, I asked for it – and I got it! "Santa!" they all shouted.

The pre-Christmas days, known as Advent, are all about coming. Of course, Advent has several aspects to it, but principally it's a period of preparation for the coming of Jesus in Bethlehem.

As we all look towards this joyous time of the year, it's true to say that people prepare for Jesus's coming in various ways.

First of all there is the world's preparation for his arrival. I think it's fair to say that there will be many challenging and even irate sermons preached this

December, and next December, and during all the Decembers to come, by ministers as they let off steam about how the world prepares for Christmas!

Be that as it may, this spectacular, celebratory, spending-spree approach has a long and very legitimate ancestry.

It's the continuation of the ancient festival of the winter solstice, when people celebrated that the sun had ceased to slide down the southern sky and made the annual turn to return it into the northern hemisphere.

This was a time of rejoicing, of good fellowship and of renewed hope, marked by good eating and drinking and by the giving and receiving of presents.

The winter solstice is on December 21 in 2022, and falls around this time each year.

We don't know exactly when Jesus was born, but December is as good a time as any, and the winter solstice seemed a better period than most to ▶

by Rev. Ian W.F. Hamilton

observe Christmas. So we can see that, despite angry sermons, the world's Advent hustle and bustle isn't entirely pagan.

And then, at the other end of the spectrum, there's God's preparation for the coming of Jesus. God was, and for ever has been, more than prepared. His Christmas countdown had well and truly begun, long in advance.

God truly wanted Israel, his chosen nation, to be ready for the coming of the world's Saviour.

As far back as 700 years before the birth of Jesus, God moved the prophet Isaiah to say to the people, "Prepare ye the way of the Lord!"

Maybe you remember the hit song of the same name from the Lloyd Webber musical, "Jesus Christ Superstar"?

Then, much later on, God sent John the Baptist to echo Isaiah's words about being prepared and being ready for Jesus's coming.

You just can't read the Bible without being made aware, time and time again, that the Messiah, the world's Saviour, was coming.

When the great moment arrived, that great hinge on which all history swings, God's eternal plan became evident, proving itself a plan that clearly involved two rather surprising characteristics.

Firstly, God chose an unlikely way in which to reveal one who was none other than himself.

He chose the child of two very ordinary people in what was then a small village in the Middle East.

Secondly, God gave a surprising message to accompany this special child's birth, namely, "Peace on earth, goodwill to men", at a time when there was considerable tension in that land.

God got ready for Jesus's coming by giving people hope. He gave hope from a renewed confidence that he did care for them.

In abstract terms, someone once put it like this: "The eternal broke into time once again, in a manger cradle".

How painstakingly God prepared. The coming of the world's Saviour was written repeatedly and indelibly throughout scripture, and if the people weren't ready for his coming, then it wasn't God's fault.

We have glanced at the world's preparation in these pre-Christmas days, and at God's preparation for the great event, but we must consider Christian preparation for the coming of Jesus, and for Christmas, as we edge towards this joyful time.

How should those of us who follow the Christian way prepare?

We must ever remember that we are in the world, therefore we share in the culture, in the semi-Christian observance of the solar turn of the year, and recognise it with joy and eager enthusiasm!

Santa Claus, parties, stockings hung by the fireplace, decorated trees and the exchanging of gifts. Each December all of these things are part and parcel for us all.

But we are also part of the

Church, therefore we must seek to understand just what God was trying to do over 2,000 years ago.

We truly must do this so that we can prepare ourselves properly for a proper Christmas observance.

So how do we properly prepare for the coming of Jesus Christ?

For those who are able, there's no better way to prepare than coming to church to engage in the Advent worship and prayer.

For those who are unable to be present in church for Advent worship, it is perfectly possible to pray and worship at home.

As someone has said, "Our homes are in a real and important sense the places of worship."

It is there, in our homes or in our sanctuaries, that we can pray primarily that throughout all the glitter and glamour of the season, the Christ of Bethlehem may find room in the hearts of our families, our communities, our country and our world. Not least may he find room in the hearts of ourselves!

The world prepares in its way, God has prepared in his unique way, and if Christian people prepare in an eager, joyful, expectant and prayerful way, then they and those around them will have a happy and blessed Christmas. ■

Nature's Calendar For *Winter*

The musk ox is well equipped for the harsh Arctic winter, with two coats that help it comfortably withstand temperatures as low as -40 degrees Celsius.

The winterberry is a deciduous holly. It drops its leaves in winter, but its berries remain, looking cheerful against any lying snow.

Winter aconites are hardy perennials that flower before almost everything else. They're practically maintenance-free, and spread naturally in an area after planting.

In 2015-2016, Russia experienced its warmest winter in 200 years of records, with temperatures 12 degrees above average. Flowers started to bloom early, and some bears even awoke from hibernation in zoos.

Ice storms are characterised by freezing rain, heavy precipitation that immediately freezes and encases all it touches in ice. In some parts of the US they're known as "glaze events".

The wolverine is a hardy animal that looks like a bear but is part of the weasel family. During winter, it can travel 15 miles a day looking for food.

Special Visitor

It's freezing out – draw up a chair, I've made a pot of soup.
Kick off those muddy welly boots, let's warm up and regroup!
I'm sure you're tired and hungry now – the table's set for two;
I hope you like fresh, crusty bread – I baked it just for you!
And when you're warm and ready, we'll sit and have a chat;
You'll tell your gran your gossip, and have pudding after that!
Yes, I've made your favourite: apple crumble's on the way.
Why wouldn't I pull out the stops? My grandchild's here to stay!

Judy Jarvie.

A Ferry Ride In Winter

The final bustle on the wharf,
The whistle's leaving blast;
Children cheer, which makes us smile,
And we are off at last!

I clutch the frosted, icy rail,
The ferry quickens pace;
The wind is ruffling all our hair
And salt spray chills the face.

Strong winds are buffeting the gulls,
Which soar above the swell;
A buoy, its sound muffled by the wind,
Clangs out its lonely knell.

With frozen cheeks and tangled hair,
We feel joyous and free,
And for that precious space of time,
At one with wind and sea!

Eileen Hay.

Rain On Remembrance Day

It rained down hard on Remembrance Day,
Drenching the parade as it made its way.
Pipers and soldiers gathered at the Cenotaph –
Names carved in stone, their for ever epitaph.
For those who have fallen, paid the ultimate price,
We gathered there, to honour their noble sacrifice.
I looked at their names, wondered about their lives,
Thinking of their families, their grief-stricken wives.
Their legacy lives on, echoing down the years,
Mother Nature agreed, with her rain-soaked tears.

Sharon Haston.

Our Piano

Our piano's been in the family for three generations or more.
It takes pride of place in the corner, though it doesn't quite match
    our décor.
I know it's a little old-fashioned, but we love it and treat it with care.
With its dark shiny wood and smiley white keys, it's a comfort just
    knowing it's there.

I see Grandad, merry and not quite in tune, trying to get us to sing,
Gran fussing around with a coaster, so his beer glass does not leave
    a ring.
They're long gone now, but the memories remain in this old piano,
    because
It's still right at the heart of our family, just as it always was.

On the top there's a clock and a pot plant, and photos in big silver
    frames,
And the lidded stool comes in handy, for storing our jigsaws and
    games.
Dad strokes it each time he passes, Mum polishes it every day.
It's a shame we can't hear it make music, 'cause not one of us
    knows how to play!

Vivien Brown.

Winter In The Churchyard

It's like a real-life Christmas card,
All glittering in the frozen air,
White sparkling moss on frost-rimed stones,
The mistletoe on trees now bare.
The holly's glossy green stands out,
Its berries glowing vibrant red,
To match the robin's cheerful breast,
As he hops around with bobbing head.
An angel statue stands serene,
Her robes seem scarcely to suffice,
Glazed as she is, in ice-cold frost –
Transfixed in stone, transfixed in ice.

Eileen Hay.

That Secret Ingredient

Add to chicken pie, a little anchovy.
Add to bread, a little beer.
Add to chocolate cake, a little mustard.
And for true love, a little tear.

Add to mushrooms, a little hoisin.
Add to chicory, a little pear.
Add to parsnips, a little honey.
And for true love, a little care.

Add to sticky ribs, a little cola.
Add to lentils, a little lime.
Add to tortellini, a little vinegar.
And for true love, a little time.

C.P. Nield.

The Lonely Christmas Tree

Snow fell from the night sky on a hillside white and bare,
On a lovely little Christmas tree, miles from anywhere.
It felt so cold and lonely, you never would believe –
For no-one wants to be alone, not when it's Christmas Eve.

And as it stood there shivering, it lifted up an eye,
And saw a shining silver star up in the cold night sky.
Said the little tree, "Oh, Christmas star, don't leave me all alone,
I wish someone would care for me and take me to their home."

The Christmas star beamed brightly and remembered with a glow,
How it shone upon a lonely stable, so many years ago.
Its voice rang through the snowflakes, "Don't worry, little tree,
For I am old and very wise – leave it all to me".

Then the Christmas star began to shine with a glow so very
    bright
That it lit up all the hillside and drove away the night.
As time stood still on that wintry hill, a glorious sight to see;
A shaft of silver star light fell on that lonely Christmas tree.

On the hilltop came a shepherd, plodding homeward through the
    snow.
When his eye fell on the Christmas tree, its branches all aglow,
He said, "On such a night as this, no-one should be alone."
And, guided by the Christmas star, he took the small tree home.

And soon the shepherd's humble house was filled with happy
    sounds.
The children dressed the little tree with presents all around.
And as the fire glowed brightly, as brightly as can be,
The star winked through the window at the happy little tree.

So if you know somebody who is lonely, sad or old,
Be like that humble shepherd, and don't leave them in the cold.
Invite them to your fireside and you very soon will see,
That you will make them happy, like that lonely Christmas tree.

Dave Dutton.

Keep The Spirit Alive

"CHRISTMAS decorations get prettier every year," my friend Katrina observed as we chanced to run into each other in town a week before the big day.

The stores were bright with their festive displays; coloured lights twinkled in the marketplace, while tinsel stars glittered in the shop window we'd paused to admire.

Katrina waved a hand at the array of Christmas tree baubles.

"I hang up my old favourites – the cardboard snowmen the children made years ago, and a spun-glass peacock that belonged to my grandma. But I can never resist treating myself to one or two brand-new decorations each year.

"The drawback," she added, laughing, "is that it's always such a miserable job to take them down again on Twelfth Night. At least, I always found it so, until last year."

I was concerned.

"What happened last year?" I asked. "Did things go so badly that you were glad when it was over?"

"The opposite." She smiled. "We had a lovely time. Even the weather was perfect, with enough snow to be pretty, but not enough to make life difficult.

"So when it came time to take down the Christmas tree and put away the ornaments, it seemed sadder than usual – as if nothing nice would ever happen again."

She caught my puzzled look.

"So you're wondering what happened to change my attitude? Well, the answer is me. I changed my own attitude.

"Let's get coffee and I'll explain."

The café was warm and bustling, and the gingerbread latte and spiced biscuits were just the thing to keep out the chill.

I became ever more intrigued by Katrina's words.

"It was while I was putting the nativity figures into their wrappings that it occurred to me to try to work out just what makes any Christmas so special.

"Candles and carols are ▶

by Maggie Ingall

lovely, and festive food is a treat – but none of those things hold the real essence of Christmas.

"The real essence is in people, and the way we behave during the festive season. It's about giving and sharing, and showing that we care about other people.

"It's about making that extra effort to see our family, and putting the most effort into forgetting old differences!

"It's about keeping in touch with distant friends, or making sure we have a smile for passing strangers."

She beamed.

"I realised that none of those things have to be limited to Christmas, so there was absolutely no reason why I couldn't carry on doing them throughout the year."

As I caught the bus home, her words played over in my mind.

Putting away the Christmas decorations rarely comes high on the list of anyone's favourite jobs.

The abrupt departure of fairy lights and sparkle can make rooms look very dismal, and definitely doesn't inspire the sort of positive thinking and feeling with which we all hope to start the New Year.

But I had been inspired by my conversation with Katrina. That evening I started making a mental list.

Why leave a room looking drab, when it could be immediately cheered by the addition of bright sprays of winter jasmine or shining posies of snowdrops?

What else had Katrina said?

Nice food, and giving and sharing.

I wouldn't be baking Christmas puddings in the next few months, but I would be making goodies that I could share with friends or take round to neighbours.

Then there was keeping in touch with those we don't see very often.

I thought of the several chatty letters that had come through my door along with Christmas cards.

I had intended to reply to them properly, but with so many other festive jobs to be done, most of the missives had been answered with a hurriedly scribbled note.

But why should keeping in touch be confined only to December?

Indeed, once the demands of Christmas are over, there is more time to get back in touch with old friends and distant relatives, whether that is by letter or over long and leisurely phone calls.

By then, it would no longer be a chore, but a positive pleasure!

As for the "smile for strangers" that Katrina mentioned . . .

Once more I reflected on my own behaviour over the last few weeks, as I had scurried along, head down, my mind preoccupied by festive deadlines and shopping lists.

I was reasonably sure that I had been polite, but not, I suspected, particularly smiley.

Well, that could certainly be remedied, and I determined it would be.

Why not? After all, a smile cheers not only the recipient, but also the giver!

I contemplated my list with satisfaction, and was reminded of that most beloved novel, Charles Dickens's "A Christmas Carol".

What was it that Scrooge said?

"I will honour Christmas in my heart and try to keep it all the year. I will live in the Past, the Present and the Future. The Spirits of all Three shall strive within me.

"I will not shut out the lessons that they teach!"

I don't know if I should thank Charles Dickens or Katrina for opening my eyes to the fact that Christmas spirit doesn't have to be wrapped up and put away along with the decorations.

Tinsel and baubles and candles and fairy lights are pretty, yet they are only external fripperies.

But a joyful and generous outlook on the world?

That's for life – not just for Christmas! ∎

Nature's Calendar For *Winter*

Snow can be good for conifers. A blanketing on the ground actually insulates the soil from freezing, meaning the tree can still draw up water.

Short-eared owls are best spotted in winter, hunting at dawn and dusk. They fly low over the bare fields, looking for small mammals such as voles.

Oymyakon is the coldest permanently settled place. In winter it can reach temperatures of -60 degrees Celsius – cold enough to freeze a bucket of hot water thrown into the air before it hits the ground.

The mountains of Honshu in Japan experience some of the highest snowfall in the world. It's most obvious on the "snow corridor", a highway kept clear by cutting a channel through the incredible accumulations.

Ptarmigans are known for their white winter plumage. During winter they also develop "pectinations", extra foot feathers that act like snowshoes, keeping their feet warm and helping them walk across snow.

The city of Montreal has over 20 miles of underground tunnels connecting it during heavy winter weather. There are restaurants, shops and metro stations down there, and an estimated half a million people use them every day in the winter.

Snow Day

Today the snow is falling fast.
As white flakes fill the sky,
I watch – all warm and snug inside –
Just glad I'm home and dry.
The forecast's for a cold spell,
More snow is on the way.
I've cancelled my appointments;
I'll go another day!
I hate to drive in snowstorms,
Icy roads are not my friend,
So I'll just stay at home today,
Until this snow storm ends.
My snow day won't be idle;
There's lots for me to do,
While watching snowflakes drift and dance,
Upon my snowbound view!

Judy Jarvie.

169

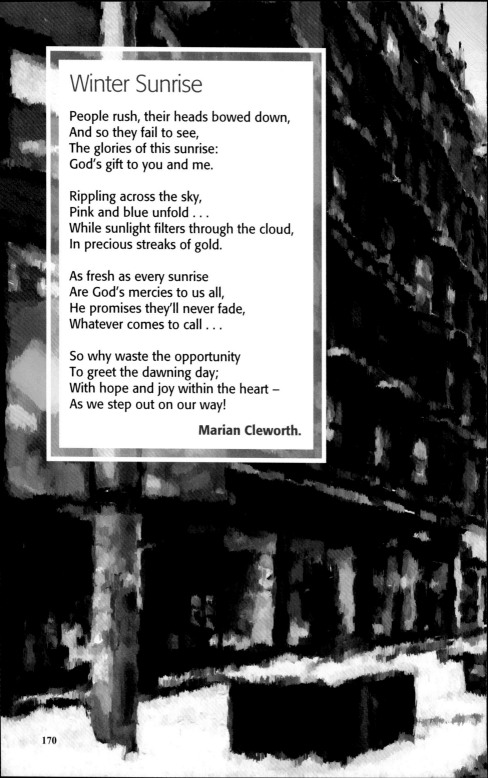

Winter Sunrise

People rush, their heads bowed down,
And so they fail to see,
The glories of this sunrise:
God's gift to you and me.

Rippling across the sky,
Pink and blue unfold . . .
While sunlight filters through the cloud,
In precious streaks of gold.

As fresh as every sunrise
Are God's mercies to us all,
He promises they'll never fade,
Whatever comes to call . . .

So why waste the opportunity
To greet the dawning day;
With hope and joy within the heart –
As we step out on our way!

Marian Cleworth.

New Year

Another year is over,
A new one soon to come;
It often feels like life's fast tracked,
As days to years soon run.
For New Year brings reflection,
And celebration, too,
For all the blessings life has brought,
And good times we've been through.
So we face firmly forward now,
Most thankful for the past.
May all enjoy a happy year,
As special as the last!

Judy Jarvie.

"There is nothing more truly artistic than to love people."
– Vincent van Gogh